Gymnastics

Bernie Blackall

Special thnaks to Stephanie Savas, Program Director and Owner, Broadway Gymnastics Centers.

Heinemann Library
Des Plaines, Illinois

First published in the United States by Heinemann Library,
an imprint of Reed Educational & Professional Publishing,
1350 East Touhy Avenue, Suite 240 West
Des Plaines, IL 60018

02 01 00 99 98
10 9 8 7 6 5 4 3 2 1

The publisher would like to thank Amanda Bledsoe and Sheena Cantu for their assistance.

Series cover and text design by Karen Young
Paged by Jo Pritchard
Cover by Smarty-pants Design
Cover photographs by Mike Liles and Bernie Blackall
Edited by Jane Pearson
Illustrations by Vasja Koman
Production by Cindy Smith
Film separations by Impact Printing Pty Ltd
Printed in Hong Kong by Wing King Tong

Library of Congress Cataloging-in-Publication Data

Blackall, Bernie, 1956-
      Gymnastics / Bernie Blackall.
         p.   cm. -- (Top Sport)
      Includes bibliographical references (p.) and index.
      Summary: Introduces gymnastics, discussing its history, American
highlights, skills, stretching exercises, equipment, events, and safety aspects.
      ISBN 1-57572-704-8 (lib. bdg.)
      1. Gymnastics--Juvenile literature. [1. Gymnastics.] I. Title.
      II. Series: Blackall, Bernie, 1956- Top Sport.
      GV461.B53   1998
      796.44--dc21   98-19585
                                                            CIP
                                                            AC

Acknowledgments
Special thanks to Eliza Fettes, Highett Youth Club, Madeleine Kim Blackall, Emily Jane Blackall, Paisley Ross, Amanda Bledsoe, Sheena Cantu, Kathryn Haldane and the coaches and gymnasts of Highett Youth Club, Cheltenham Youth Club and the Victorian Institute of Sport, Mentone.

Photographs supplied by:
Australian Sports Commission: p. 6. Bernie Blackall: pp. 9, 10, 11, 12, 13, 14, 15, 16, 21. Coo-ee Historical Picture Library: p. 8. Coo-ee Picture Library: pp. 5, 20 (left), 21 (top), 23. Sue and Wies Fajzullin Photography: pp. 20 (right), 27. Mike Liles: p. 17; ; Lutz Bongarts, p. 26. Sports Illustrated/Peter Read Miller, p.7; Sports Illustrated/John Iacono, p.6; Sydney Freelance, p. 24.

Some words are shown in bold, **like this.** You can find out what they mean by looking in the glossary.

Gymnastics require specialist instruction. Do not attempt any of the techniques and movements in this book without a qualified, registered instructor present.

Contents

About Gymnastics

Gymnastics combines the elements of coordination, balance, agility, strength, and grace, and involves the use of almost every part of the human body. Competitive gymnastics can be divided into two general areas:

- **artistic gymnastics**
- **rhythmic gymnastics**

Artistic gymnastics

Artistic gymnasts perform on various pieces of **apparatus** set up around the hall. Women's gymnastics involves performances on the **balance beam**, the **vaulting horse**, the **uneven parallel bars** and the **floor**. Men's gymnastics involves performances on the **pommel horse**, the **rings**, the **horizontal bar**, the **parallel bars**, the vaulting horse, and the floor. Performances on each piece of apparatus involve **routines**, or **sequences** of movements and balances, that show the gymnasts' skill, strength, and flexibility.

Artistic gymnastics are major events at the Olympic Games and attract a lot of media coverage.

Rhythmic gymnastics

Female rhythmic gymnastic events involve performances on the floor area with small hand-held apparatus—hoops, ball, rope, ribbon, and clubs. The apparatus is used to enhance ballet-like steps and gymnastic movements performed to music.

Performances on the beam require great strength, skill, and balance.

U.S. Highlights

Gymnastics is very popular in the United States. Over the past two decades there have been many successful United States gymnasts. Mary Lou Retton won a gold medal, two silvers, and two bronzes at the 1984 Olympics in Los Angeles. In the same games, the U.S. Men's team won the gold team medal. Other gymnasic stars include Kim Demeskal winning the World Championships in Indiana and Shannon Miller winning the silver medal in the 1992 Olympics held in Barcelona, Spain.

Jair Lynch

Jair Lynch was born October 2, 1971 in Amherst, Massachusetts and began studying gymnastics when he was 8 years old. At age 20, Lynch was the youngest member of the 1992 U.S. Men's Olympic Gymnastics Team, and only the second African American to compete in Olympic Gymnastics. Lynch narrowly missed a medal in the 1992 Olympics, but in Atlanta in 1996, won a silver medal on the parallel bars and become the first African American male gymnast ever to medal in the Olympics.

Jair Lynch

U.S. Women's Team

One of the most exciting recent successes for United States Gymnasts was the United State's Women's team gold medal at the 1996 Olympics in Atlanta. The team consisted of Shannon Miller, Dominique Dawes, Amanda Borden, Jaycee Phelps, Dominique Moceanu, Kerri Strug, and Amy Chow.

There were several factors that contributed tot the success in Atlanta. The members of the team had much experience at a high level of competition. They had all participated in World Championships and Dawes, Miller, and Strug had all participated in the 1992 Olympics in Barcelona. Aside from experience, one of the biggest factors was that the teammembers all really liked each other.

Kerri Strug

No one will forget the Kerry Strug's winning vault with a sprained left ankle at the 1996 Olympics in Atlanta. Her high score secured the gold medal for the team.

Following in her older sister's footsteps, Strug began gymnastics at the age of two. She entered her first competition at age eight and her progress was steady. When she was 13 she moved to Texas to train with well-known coach, Bela Karolyi. She was the youngest U.S. athlete at the 1992 Olympics in Barcelona, Spain, where she won a bronze medal. After the Olympics Karolyi retired from coaching. Kerri moved back to Tuscon and finished high school, while continuing gymnastics with three different coaches. She finished high school and had been accepted to UCLA, when she decided to compete in the 1996 Olympics, Karolyi had come out of retirement. She resumed training with him. She lived her dream of winning the gold medal in the 1996 Olympic Games.

US Gold!

History of Gymnastics

Ancient gymnastics

Ancient art indicates that forms of gymnastics were practiced 3,000 years ago in Egypt and later in Greek and Roman civilizations.

The Greeks realized the importance of keeping their soldiers fit. Training included a range of gymnastic-style activities—rope climbing, throwing, jumping, and wrestling.

Among the **apparatus** the Romans introduced was the wooden horse (vault).

Because the cavalry needed to be skilled at mounting and dismounting their horses, the wooden horse was ideal for developing these abilities.

Wandering troupes

During the Middle Ages, wandering troupes of acrobats performed tumbling, juggling, and gymnastic acts for entertainment. The 16th-century writer Rabelais described the wandering acrobats, who would erect a rope or bar between two trees "and there did swing by the hands, touching at nothing."

Modern gymnastics

During the 18th and 19th centuries, gymnastics was re-introduced into Europe. To strengthen the German army, then at war with Napoleon's French troops, Friedrich Ludwig Jahn began fitness classes. In 1811 Jahn established an outdoor gymnastics center in Berlin called the Hasenheid. He included a number of pieces of fixed apparatus in his open-air gymnasium, including **vaulting horses, horizontal bars, parallel bars,** and **rings.**

Gymnastics was included in the first modern Olympic Games in Athens in 1896. The competitions were staged in the center of the athletics track and involved 75 men from five countries.

Women's gymnastics in 1881

What You Need

Clothing

When you first begin gymnastics, you will not need any special clothing—just a T-shirt and shorts will be fine. As you improve you will require clothing that lets you stretch and move into different positions and allows your body shapes to be seen by the judges.

Girls usually wear leotards, which are stretchy and tight fitting, and allow them to move freely. Leotards let the coach see the body shape during training and make it easier to spot mistakes.

For practice or when competing on **floor** and vaulting exercises, boys wear a sleeveless leotard with shorts. On the other pieces of apparatus, they wear sleeveless leotards and long white trousers. This clothing is lightweight and flexible.

Most gymnasts, male and female, prefer to work in bare feet. Many girls work in bare feet on the **balance beam,** although some wear special beam shoes.

It is important to keep your muscles warm before and after you perform. You should wear a tracksuit for the warm-up exercises and remove it just before you perform. To keep your muscles warm, put the suit on again after your routine.

Handguards and chalk

For work on the bars and rings, gymnasts usually wear handguards (also called grips). They give gymnasts a good grip on the apparatus and help prevent blisters. Handguards also have a wrist strap to support the wrists.

Gymnasts apply **chalk** to their hands and sometimes feet. The chalk (magnesium carbonate) prevents you from slipping or sticking as you perspire.

Chalk and handguards help gymnasts grip the bars or rings, allowing the hands to move around the apparatus without sticking or slipping.

Safety

Beginners and top-level performers alike should observe the following safety rules.

• Always wear appropriate clothing—your hair should be tied back and all jewelry removed.

• Always warm up thoroughly to avoid strains and other injuries.

• When learning new activities and skills, always practice some lead-up movements before attempting the full movement. Your coach will make sure you are ready to attempt new skills by providing you with lead-up challenges.

• Never stretch or push yourself beyond what is reasonably comfortable. It is better to build up gradually to a new movement or balance than to injure yourself by pushing too hard.

• For all **apparatus** and tumbling work, be sure that mats are beneath and around the apparatus.

• Always check your equipment before performing. Remove any trolleys, benches, or other "hardware" from around the apparatus.

Spotting for safety

The **spotter's** main responsibility is to save the performer from injury. He or she must also help the performer

The spotter helps the performer to "feel" the correct movement or position and is responsible for preventing a fall.

"feel" the movement to improve on further attempts.

Here are the basics to good spotting technique.

• Give light assistance to guide the performer through the movement.

• Make sure that you are in the best position to react quickly if required.

• As a gymnast becomes confident and is performing the movement correctly, provide less assistance, but always remain in position to prevent any injuries.

Skills

You will learn a few basic skills before you progress to the various pieces of apparatus. Always warm up thoroughly before trying these movements.

Making shapes

The various shapes or positions that you are able to make with your body are the basis of gymnastics. It is important to learn to make shapes and then to move smoothly from one position to another. With extra fitness and improved technique, you will be able to achieve an ever-increasing range of shapes.

Try to be aware of all parts of your body and to feel in control of the position. Keep your muscles tense and your body "strong'"throughout the movement.

Back support

From a seated position with your hands flat on the floor beside you, tense your body and raise your hips to form a straight line from your toes to your head. Keep your chin up so that your neck is straight.

Front support

From an "all fours" position with your hands flat on the floor below your shoulders, raise your hips and extend your toes. Try to form a straight line from your toes to your head.

Front support

Back support

Skills

Balances

A **balance** is a shape that you make and hold. Balance work demands good posture. It requires excellent muscle control to maintain a still balance. Try to hold each balance for about 10 seconds, and then gently reverse the procedure to come down.

Shoulder stand balance

The shoulder stand requires good balance as well as flexibility and strength. Remember to point your toes and keep your legs stretched and straight.

Lie on the floor with your hands, palms down, beside you. Push down against the floor with your arms as you bend your knees and lift your legs. Raise your body to a firm vertical shoulder stand balance.

V-sit balance

Begin in a seated position with your body supported by your hands on the floor behind you and your toes pointed on the floor in front of you. Straighten your legs so that your toes reach up above your head. As your skill level improves raise your arms up and to the side to complete the V-sit. Keep your back as straight as you can and your chin up.

Begin the V-sit balance sitting on the floor so that your upper body and your thighs form the V. When you stretch your legs up and your arms back, your whole body will form the V.

Bridge balance

A bridge is a graceful position which combines balance with flexibility and strength. As you gain control of the position, push forward over your shoulders and keep your body straight from your hips to your toes. Children under age 6 should not perform this skill.

Lie on the floor with your knees bent and feet flat on the floor. Bend your elbows and place your hands on the floor on either side of your head.

Push up from your hands and feet raising your body into the bridge position.

Knees on elbows balance

The knees on elbows balance is an ideal means of building balance, coordination, and strength. Place your hands shoulder-width apart and lean forward so that your weight is evenly over your hands. Lift your hips and bring your feet up off the ground. Raise your hips further so that you can rest your knees on your elbows. Your hips are high and your head is about 12 inches (80 centimeters) above the mat. Hold the position for a few seconds and then gently reverse the procedure to come down.

Try to control each stage of the movement to form the balance.

Skills

Headstands

Balancing on your head and hands is an important basic gymnastics skill that you will use widely as you progress. Practice the following movements for good technique.

The tuck headstand and the toe-walk headstand are ideal ways to gain confidence and skill.

Toe-walk headstand

As you lift your hips, straighten your legs and point your toes. Keep your hips high as you "walk" your toes in until your hips are directly above your head. Push down on your hands as you raise your legs into the upright position.

Tuck headstand

Place your hands flat on the floor about shoulder-width apart. Put your forehead on the floor so that your hands and your forehead form a triangle. Lift your hips up above your head and raise your feet into the tuck position.

Once you have control of the tuck position, straighten your legs into an upright headstand.

Head and hand positions

Your forehead and hands must form a triangle on the mat. Your hands are shoulder-width apart with fingers spread. Head contact is made with the top of the forehead where your hair begins.

Each of the bases (points of the triangle) should be about 10 inches (25 centimeters) apart and your weight should be spread evenly over each base.

Handstand

The handstand is an important component of many sequences on the **floor, bar, beam, rings,** and vault. Before using it in a **sequence,** you need to be able to hold a steady upright **balance.** Practice it often with a coach or friend spotting for you.

The kick

Practice this lead-up movement to give you the right "feel" for the handstand position.

Start with your hands on the ground and arms straight. Watch the ground between your hands as you kick your legs up one after the other. As you improve, your hips will travel higher and higher until you have the "feel" for where they need to be for the correct handstand.

Once you have control of the kick, you can begin the handstand from a standing position. As you improve, you will require less assistance from your **spotter.**

Follow with your second leg and then hold your legs together, toes pointed.

Start with your arms stretched above your head. Point your leading toe and push off your back foot as you put your hands firmly on the floor, fingers spread. Keep your arms straight and your head between your arms. Look at the floor between your hands as you push off your front foot and kick up your rear leg.

Front walkover

Once you have mastered the handstand, you can attempt the front walkover. With a spotter to guide you, begin as if you were performing a handstand. Kick up a bit harder so that your leading leg travels right over your body with enough momentum to allow you to stand up as your first foot reaches the floor. Keep your legs split throughout the movement.

Skills

Jumping and leaping

Many **apparatus** activities involve jumping and landing, or leaping and landing. A **springboard** or a mini-trampoline are often used for jumping or leaping onto apparatus such as the **balance beam.** For **floor** activities, gymnasts jump and leap from the floor.

For a jump, the gymnast takes off and lands on two feet. For a leap, the gymnast takes off from one foot and lands on the other.

The springboard

The **springboard** assists you in rebounding high for vaulting, and for **mounting** other apparatus such as the balance beam. It is 50 inches (120 centimeters) long and about 8 inches (20 centimeters) high at its highest point. The springiest part of the springboard is about 8 inches (20 centimeters) from the end. You will get the best spring by jumping from this area.

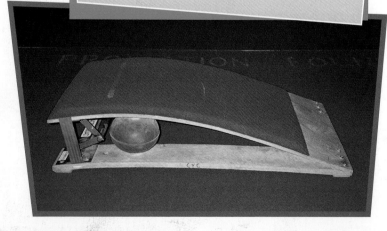

Straight jump

To become familiar with the springboard, practice the straight jump from a 10 to 16 feet (3 to 4 meter) run-up. Land firmly about 8 inches (20 centimeters) from the end of the springboard or in the middle of the mini-trampoline. Jump high with your arms raised, and land on both feet, about 20 to 35 inches (50 to 90 centimeters) in front of your takeoff point.

Star jump

As you take off, stretch your arms and legs wide at identical angles to form a symmetrical shape. Land with your feet together and arms by your side about 20 to 35 inches (50 to 90 centimeters) in front of your takeoff point.

Squat jump

Spring high from your takeoff. Bring your knees up to your chest so that at the peak of the jump you are in a tight tuck position. Aim for a high jump rather than a longer, less-controlled jump. Keep your head high with your chin up throughout the jump.

Straddle pike jump

With a straight back and extended legs, ankles, and feet, bend forward from your hips. Stretch your fingers to your toes and look ahead as you form the pike position at the peak of your jump. Land with your feet together and your arms by your side.

Hold your knees to your chest and look forward for the squat jump.

Split or stride leap

The leap is a movement where a gymnast springs from one foot to land on the opposite foot. Height and distance are important, and the overall effect is one of poise, balance, and grace. The leap is not performed using a springboard or a mini-trampoline.

The split leap is the best leap to learn first. Using a run-up to gather momentum, take off from one foot and stretch your leading foot upwards and forwards. Land on your leading foot and continue to travel forwards.

Straddle pike jump

Stretch forward but keep your head up.

Split leap

Point your toes and look up as you leap as high and as far as you can.

Skills

Rotations

Rotations, such as the forward and the backward roll, are often used in floor and **balance beam** sequences to link a variety of shapes and movements together. It is important to learn to roll correctly to achieve a smooth, controlled rotation.

Forward roll

As a beginner you will find that rolling down a slight slope helps you to learn the correct movement. Use a gymnastics wedge or a mat-covered **springboard.**

Backward roll

The backward roll is a forward roll in reverse. It requires plenty of momentum so always roll back strongly.

Start in the same squat position as for the forward roll but facing the other way. As you roll bring your hands close to your ears so that they will strike the mat in a flat position. Remember to keep your head tucked into your chest as you roll and push your hands firmly into the mat to help you bring your hips over.

Forward roll

| Start in a squat position on the balls of your feet with your arms outstretched to keep your balance. | Place your hands on the floor, tuck your head in to your chest, and push off. | Push strongly with your hands as your hips move over your shoulders—this will increase your body roll and allow you to balance back onto your feet as you come back to the squat position. | Finish in the squat position, reaching forward with both arms. |

Events

Artistic gymnastics

Artistic gymnasts move around the gymnasium performing sequence routines on each piece of **apparatus.**

Floor

The floor event takes place on the 40x40 foot (12x12 meter) cushioned mat. It involves a sequence of movements and balances that flow together to make the **routine.**

Cartwheels

Cartwheels can be used in sequences to link other movements such as jumps or flips. To complete a good cartwheel, you should travel in a straight line, and your body should move through a vertical plane.

Cartwheel

| Lift one leg high and straight in front, with your toe pointed. | Bend down to put one hand on the floor as your rear leg moves up. | Bring your hips over and place your second hand on the mat. | Keep your body straight so that your hips travel directly above your shoulders. | Push off the floor with your first hand as your leading foot comes down to the floor. | Finish with your feet apart and your arms out straight. |

Events

Balance beam

The balance beam routine is performed only by women. The beam is 5 inches (13 centimeters) wide and 16 feet (5 meters) long, and the height of the beam is adjustable. The balance beam routine lasts between 45 and 90 seconds. It involves a sequence of movements including jumps, turns, leaps, and acrobatic skills, as well as balance positions. Gymnasts are free to move forwards, backwards, or sideways on the beam. As you become more confident on the beam, you will begin to perform the skills you have learned on the floor.

Begin your beam work on a low beam or bench. When your movements become more controlled and you gain confidence, you can progress to a standard beam that is surrounded by safety mats.

Arabesque

The arabesque, a graceful ballet-like position, is a commonly used balance in women's gymnastics. While balancing on one leg, lean forward with your arms stretched out to the side and bring your other leg up behind you.

V-sit

A routine on the balance beam must include some low moves, such as the V-sit. On the beam, you can do the V-sit with both legs stretching up or with one leg bent. From the V-sit, you can push back into a backward roll or push up into a bridge.

To hold a good V-sit, keep your head up and stretch your leg upwards. Hold the beam firmly with your thumbs across the top of the beam and your fingers pointing down the sides. Keep your toes pointed, and stretch your leg high.

When doing an arabesque, try to bring your leg up as high as possible. Top-level gymnasts can reach an almost vertical position.

Rings

The **rings** are used only by male gymnasts. Gymnasts need great strength not only to swing themselves high over the rings, but also to hold the rings in the position required for the movements. The USAG has a low-level competitive program for younger boys, and they compete on the rings.

Performers are not permitted to swing the rings as they move their bodies into different positions. Only the gymnast's hands may touch the **apparatus.**

There are some basic positions and moves that you will learn first—the **hang** position, the front and back support positions, and the controlled body swing. Your coach will support you and help you get the feel of the correct positions.

The rings require more strength than any other piece of apparatus.

Concentrate on keeping the rings steady as you hold the positions. Hold your body firm, and keep your legs straight and your toes pointed. As your skill level increases, you will be able to combine the basic positions and moves into a rings **routine.**

Front support

Hang position

Back support

Events

Vault

The vault, included in both men's and women's routines, is the shortest event, lasting only seconds. Gymnasts run up and travel over the vault using various styles of jumps. A run-up of 50 to 82 feet (15 to 25 meters) is used to gain speed, while the takeoff jump from the **springboard** gives the gymnast height and further forward momentum.

Squat vault

The squat vault involves tucking your feet through between your arms as you travel over the vault. For a good lead-up exercise, stand on the springboard with your hands on the top of the vault, shoulder-width apart. Jump off the springboard and land on the vault in the squat position. Then stretch upwards as you jump off. As you master the movement, add a run-up and then progress to the squat jump.

Straddle vault

The straddle vault involves stretching the legs wide apart to clear the vault. Run up and take off as for the squat vault. As you place your hands on the top of the vault, lift your hips high and stretch your legs out to the sides. Bring your legs back together to land with your feet together on the other side.

Squat vault

Run hard and jump off the springboard. Stretch out and place your hands shoulder-width apart on the top of the vault.

Tuck your knees into the squat position as you swing your hips through between your arms. Stretch your arms up high as you leave the vault and land in an upright position with your arms by your side.

Pommel horse

The **pommel horse** is similar to the **vaulting horse,** but it has two handles, known as pommels, attached to the top. The pommel horse is a men's-only event, where gymnasts swing their legs high over and around the horse, supporting themselves with one or two hands on the pommels. The routine lasts about 25 seconds and is a great test of skill and strength.

Three support positions—front, straddle, and back—form the basis of pommel horse work.

The gymnast may touch the horse only with his hands.

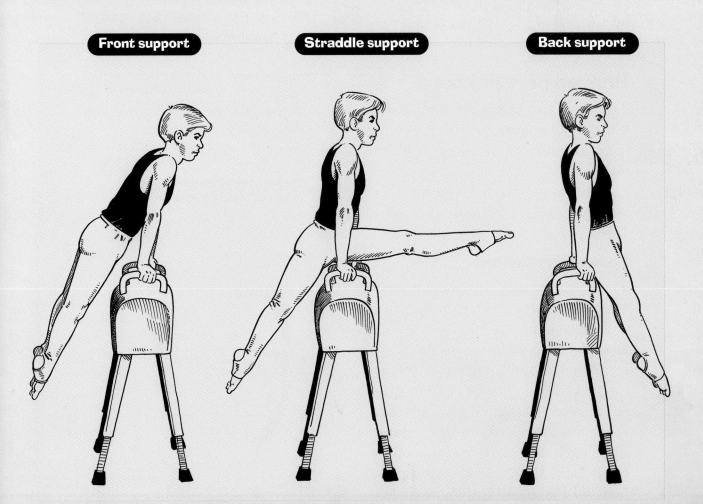

Front support **Straddle support** **Back support**

Events

Bars

There are three kinds of bar **apparatus:** the **horizontal bar** and the **parallel bars** for men and the **uneven parallel bars** for women. Each one requires strong arms and shoulders as the gymnasts swing over and around the bars for their routines. Beginners often train above a foam-filled pit or thick "skill cushion" that allows them to practice maneuvers without injury should they fall.

The uneven parallel bars routine is performed at high speed, and requires perfect coordination, strength, and skill.

Uneven parallel bars

This apparatus consists of two parallel horizontal bars, one at a height of about 5 feet (1.5 meters), the other at about 7.5 feet (2.3 meters). A **routine** on these bars includes swings, circles, handstand positions, and release and catch moves. It is a popular event with spectators.

Forward rotation

The forward rotation from the lower bar is a good movement to learn first. Begin in a front support position with your hips against the bar and your weight supported on straight arms. Your hands should be facing forwards as they grip the bar. Loosen your grip slightly as you rotate forward. Once you have completed a half circle, and your head is pointing down to the floor, extend your legs and body for the second half of the circle.

Land with both feet together on the floor and your knees slightly bent as you release your grip of the bar.

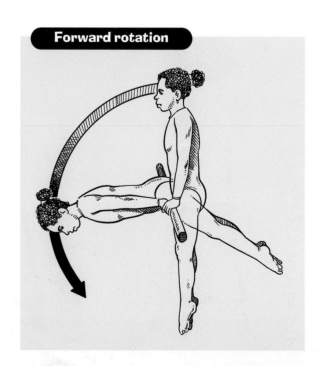

Forward rotation

Horizontal bar

The **horizontal bar** is a single bar about 9 feet above the mat. It is a men's event, and routines include spectacular full circles, release and grab moves, and spinning and somersaulting dismounts.

The most common beginners' exercise on the horizontal bar is the basic swing. With a coach assisting and spotting, begin your swing standing on a **vaulting horse.** Stretch forward to the bar. Keep your head upright between your elbows and push your hips forward, with toes pointed. Your body should be in a straight line at all times. Swing back to land on the vaulting horse.

Parallel bars

The **parallel bars** are two wooden bars, 16.5 inches (42 centimeters) apart and 6.4 feet (1.95 meters) above the floor. It is a men's event where gymnasts move above and between the bars supported by one or both hands. The parallel bars routine calls for a wide variety of skills including supports, hangs, swings, balances, and strength moves.

There are three support positions to learn before beginning to build up a routine. They are the straight arm support, the upper arm support, and the hang support. For each one, your coach or a spotter will help you get into position. Practice holding the support until you feel fully in control of the position.

Straight arm support

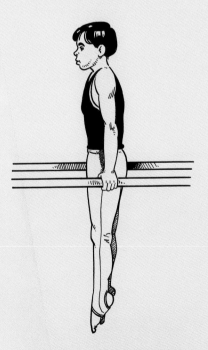

Upper arm support

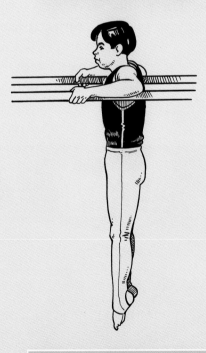

Hang support

Keeping your arms straight and your body rigid, support yourself over the bars. Hold your chin up and look straight ahead.

With your arms bent, grip the bars with your hands and support your body with your upper arms pushing down on the bars.

Hang from the bars with your arms straight and your body bent at the hips so that your torso and legs are parallel with the bars. Keep your head in line with your body.

Events

Scoring and judging artistic gymnastics

Gymnasts perform compulsory and optional **routines** on each piece of **apparatus.** A compulsory routine is made up of a set series of movements that each gymnast must complete. For the optional routine, each gymnast chooses the movements for his or her performance.

A panel of judges scores each routine out of a maximum 10 points. The points allotted depend on:

• the degree of difficulty of the movements in the routine

• how well the movements are performed.

Gymnasts lose points for mistakes or for any element of an exercise not performed correctly. Judges also consider the flow of the routine — how smoothly the various elements are linked.

Top gymnasts must be capable on each piece of apparatus because at the end of competition the scores from each compulsory and optional routine are added. The gymnast with the highest total wins.

A team competition involves six gymnasts on each team. On each piece of apparatus each team's top five scores are recorded—the winning team is the one with the highest overall score.

A panel of judges scores each routine.

Rhythmic gymnastics

Rhythmic gymnastics is performed by girls and women. It is similar to the women's floor event of artistic gymnastics. Each routine is performed to music, using dance steps adapted from ballet in combination with gymnastic movements. Routines last 60 to 90 seconds and are performed on a 40x40 foot (12x12 meter) carpeted mat. Since it made its first appearance at the Los Angeles Olympic Games in 1984, rhythmic gymnastics has become very popular.

There are five pieces of **apparatus**—the ribbon, the hoop, the rope, the ball, and the hand clubs. Each piece of apparatus is used as an artistic feature of the routine as well as to complement the body shapes and movements of the gymnasts. With practice you will learn to be proficient with each.

Team events, with six gymnasts to a team, are also held. Members of the team perform together with their choice of apparatus.

The ribbon

The satin ribbon is approximately 20 feet (6 meters) long and is attached to a wooden or bamboo stick. Skills include swings, circles, spirals, figure 8s and throws.

The hoop

Gymnasts swing the hoop in various ways: turning it, rolling and rotating it, throwing and catching it, and even passing themselves through it.

The ribbon routine requires the gymnast to match her movements with those of the ribbon. The ribbon must be moving at all times.

The rope

The main feature of rope work is skipping, but it can be used in a variety of movements. It can be thrown high so that it stands straight in the air, and then caught again as it falls. It can also be swung to enhance many movements and balances.

The ball

The ball can be bounced, rolled, thrown, and caught. It cannot be held, only carefully balanced on the hand. Gymnasts toss it up and roll it across their bodies as they perform their movements and balances.

The hand clubs

The two wooden or plastic clubs, each between 18 and 20 inches (40 and 50 centimeters) long, give the gymnasts the opportunity to display their skills of throwing and catching, swinging, twirling, and circling the clubs as they perform their movements and balances.

Getting Ready

Before attempting any gymnastic activity, you must warm up to prevent injury. Warm-up exercises increase your heart rate and your breathing rate as well as loosen your muscles and joints to get you ready for gymnastics movements.

Jog or walk for 3 to 5 minutes to increase your body temperature and heart rate. Once your body has warmed up, the following stretches will increase your flexibility.

Repeat each exercise four times on each side of the body. Hold each stretch for between 10 and 15 seconds and then relax the muscle before the next exercise.

Arm and shoulder stretch
Bend your arm behind your head and gently push your elbow down with your other hand.

Shoulder stretch
Stretch one arm straight across your body. Use your other hand to pull your elbow in to your chest until you feel the stretch.

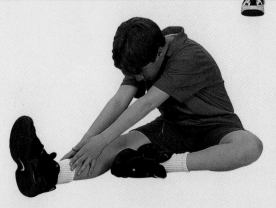

Hamstring and lower back stretch
Sit on the floor with one leg stretched out straight in front. Your other leg is bent so that your foot touches the knee of your straight leg. Reach forward towards your toes keeping your back as straight as possible.

Arm circles
Stretch your arms above your head and then take them around in circles forwards and then backwards, stretching as far up and around as you can.

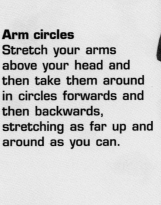

Quadriceps stretch
Hold a wall, beam, or a partner with one hand for balance. Bend one knee and pull your foot up behind you.

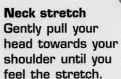

Calf stretch
Stand with one foot about 3 feet (1 meter) in front of the other. Bend your leading leg and lean forward, keeping both feet flat on the floor.

Neck stretch
Gently pull your head towards your shoulder until you feel the stretch.

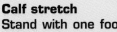

Lower back stretch
Lie on your back with your legs outstretched. Bend one knee up to your chest and lift your head and shoulders off the floor to meet it.

Taking it Further

USA Gymnastics
Pan American Plaza
201 South Capitol Ave. Suite 300
Indianapolis, IN 46225
phone: (317) 237-5050
fax: (317) 237-5069

Publications:

USA Gymnastics Magazine
Pan American Plaza
201 S. Capitol Ave., Suite 300
Indianapolis, IN 46225

International Gymnast Magazine
P.O. Box 721020
Norman, OK 73070

More Books to Read

Armentrout, David. *Gymnastics*. Vero Beach, FL: The Rourke Book Company, Inc. 1997.

Cohen, Joel H. *Superstars of Women's Gymnastics*. New York: Chelsea House Publishers. 1997.

Jensen, Julie. *Beginning Gymnastics*. Minneapolis, MN: Lerner Publishing Group. 1995.

Maurer, Tracy. *Rhythmic Gymnastics*. Vero Beach, FL: Rourke Press, Inc. 1997.

Normile, Dwight. *Gymnastics*. Chatham, NJ: Raintree Steck-Vaughn. 1996.

Rambeck, Richard. *The U. S. Women's Gymnastics Team*. Chicago: Child's World Inc. 1997.

Glossary

apparatus equipment used in gymnastics

artistic gymnastics competition for men and women on the floor, balance beam, vault, uneven parallel bars, parallel bars, horizontal bar, rings, pommel horse

balance to hold a position or body shape

balance beam a piece of artistic gymnastics equipment that women perform on

chalk magnesium carbonate, applied to hands and feet to prevent them from sticking or slipping

floor the floor is an artistic gymnastic event where women and men perform sequences of movements and balances

hang when a gymnast is suspended below the apparatus by the hands

horizontal bar a piece of gymnastic apparatus. The horizontal bar is a single bar, more than 6.5 feet above the floor

mounting the method by which the gymnast jumps onto the apparatus to begin the routine

parallel bars a piece of artistic gymnastic equipment, consisting of two parallel horizontal bars

pommel horse a piece of gymnastic apparatus very similar to the vault but with two handles called pommels on top

rhythmic gymnastics a women's-only gymnastics discipline that combines the use of small hand-held apparatus (e.g., ribbons) with gymnastic movements

rings a piece of artistic gymnastics apparatus consisting of two wooden rings suspended from the ceiling

rotations movement in a full circle, forwards or backwards

routine a sequence of movements and balances on a piece of apparatus

sequence a number of gymnastics movements and balances performed one after the other in a routine

spotter person who helps a gymnast perform a movement or balance. The spotter's job is to prevent injury and to help the gymnast feel the correct movement or position.

springboard a piece of equipment that gymnasts jump on to give them spring for vaulting and for mounting other apparatus

uneven parallel bars a piece of artistic gymnastics equipment. The bars are parallel but at different heights.

vaulting horse a piece of artistic gymnastics apparatus. Male and female gymnasts perform spectacular skills through various positions over the vault.

Index